NUDITY

Back cover photo: Aaron Alpert
Cover design: Elyse Cizek

ISBN-13:978-0692731253 (Victory)
ISBN-10:0692731253

To every girl who has broken her own heart once
or twice.

Jameson Bottle Green and Other Colors

Jameson Bottle Green and Other Colors

There's a sick and funny
humming
there's a funny sort
of strumming to beats
unkempt by the sorcerer's heat
locking drawers and hiding keys
The fog that forms in
silent formations
around secrets unworthy
of the vibration of breath
quiets all but the mind
in times
of countless screaming cries
for forgiveness
The bottle lies heavy in
weighted lies of weight
Truly
as forgotten truths follow
framed friendships in fear
My dear
syntax and satin
between plump lips
and crooked teeth
rimmed glasses
left empty on smooth glass
for ashing
The title of tidal waves crashing against
my inner skin
the process of lashes
of tongues kept sweet
and only for me
In a forest kept only for the trees

Everything You Need to Know

Oh the taste
of ones own words
on her own lips
for her own thoughts
to dance patterns of her
own face
in her own pace
and cadence
is the joy of the writer
as loser of pens
in delight of the poet
in her own horizons

Softening her skin in baths
of her own lapping tongue
licking more than her wounds
soothing coos sung
of her own lullabies
and folding pages lengthwise
to tuck her words
in books she finds
on shelves outside herself

Narcissism and self pleasure
pave roads
to the treasure
of a captivated crowd
held down in the author's delight
of the sight of them
The ones who wear
her words like secret codes
tattooed in her flows
and her slurs

those of whom she writes
her secrets
into pieces meek in regret
Fear of being exposed
were they ever to question
or judge her intentions

In arrogance and grandeur
and a slick of red lipstick
may her cleverness never
fall deaf to her critics
and may she try less to fix it
but instead to dig
deeper in truth
and refuse
to leave her stanzas eccentric
or obtuse.

May each piece construct
a beginning, middle and end
and may her reader meddle
and pretend
or search between sinnings
and losses and fend
for themselves in the
resources she so
carefully sorts

And in short
may she reach you
and touch a part you hadn't found
in rounded verses of rhythm
bound to a breech of
color in sound as
she sees it.

For when she reads it
it is not just a series of words,
but a watercolor of nouns and verbs
in carefully enunciated
pronunciations of hue.
And all she wishes is
to share her view.

Matted Red Carpet

Danny's Room

What am I
but a collection
of tiny mirrors
reflecting back
upon all
open eyes
what it is I see

Were there not
a light to refract
to shine upon
those hiding
in dark back rooms
who would look
upon me

in sticky concrete
painted floors
and stale cigarettes
ashed in votives
we construct and
perform our motives

in dancing and
shaking hands
and exchanging
glances just
searching for
ourselves in
our own lands

finding only
our fleshy reflections

and sweat and
rejection
desperately seeking
a mirror into
what we know
must be our best

that we could
not of course
be one
like the rest
in a sea of faces
in facets
of the same
spinning ball

gatherers in random
tandem all in
this scene
where scoundrels
would never
nor could
they stand to be

of course for
we are tied
to no creed
derived in the
lives of those
in need
independent
of sin or disease

Superior in
status we are
the freest of free

to dance
and smoke
without care
for we know better
than to stare

into mirrors
reflecting
the me or we
or grow keen
to whence
our celebration
becomes darkness
dim in apathy

West Temple

Once I preferred to watch
as my feet followed whomever
first footed the path before me

That once when the light was
never so bright
to read the intentions of eyes
hooded in intoxicated ideals
for where my last step might be

where dancing heels and bending
knees jumped to the beat
when the music
called for obedience
in the mirror refracted
lines of white light

I danced on matted red rugs
dampened with spilled sweat
and pickled meat
Rotting in hidden
corners, forgotten in the night

I lubricated my willingness
to say things like no
or cloud it more likely
or pausing it entirely
in scarlet shades of when not
to partake so politely

And This Was the Last Time

Once in a mirror
I discovered my skin
covered in
cracking packed sand
and the driest of parchment
without the nobility
of a tale in fresh ink
telling the story of a dignity
not even one destroyed
Instead barren
as the desert sands blew
in mid-morning light
nothing could quench
or make mud of the dirt
in sunshine champagne rust
as my mortar turned to dust.

Lover

Oh her legs
and her sweet stink
the way she lingered
on my lips
and my teeth

She only spoke in lies
and laid with me
on cold winter nights
entangled as one
she was within me

Her smooth touch
and fever flushed
dry and chocolate
the way she hurt
too much to leave

Never a boundary.
She never teased.
I took her all in.
Night after sour sweet
night she sang to me

Mmm and her breath
before she met my lips
I inhaled of her
oh darling in my air, my
care of her never shared

No longer she is mine
and her kiss I must deny
for fear of her,

as I will never again
drink of her
blood red
red wine.

Nebula: A Poem for Lily

the gentle
rustle of ice in
my whiskey
two bitters
is honest

or a consequential link
between casual spitting
and loose rocking
or locked jaws

when 'enough'
had been lost in 'yes'
or the taste of ripe rot
on breath in the
absence of sense

tossing suggestions
wild and passionate
high cheekbones dancing
with closed eyes

when the muscles know more
than the mind or
maybe slower
more slowly
as it happens knowingly

lemon tight lips
sipping one last
to maybe relax
or perhaps

that one last knock
or bump bump
might create a new path
a not really quite
relapse

over passing gaze of strangers
one key might
a specific haphazard
combination unlock

crying out in vain
to some great visionary
or a god
who stopped listening
when first it heard 'yes'

accidental permission
in missionary positions
submitting and allowance
on a quest for pure visions blessed

undressed pause
to hastily redress
in wrinkles and soil
and the paralyzing weight
of starting again with less

and the glass
will empty
and truly digress
but of course we were just being honest

Cream and Honey Sweet

All Black

It's not as if
I ache for you or I
lie on my stomach
waiting or holding my
breath for the hours in
between your texts.

Though the tightening of my
chest as you approach
leaves room for
the fantasy of you
at my breast.

I find myself listening
too hard to the whispering
gnat fly in my ear
and her cry to put
this to rest.

That voice, that,
avoidance of your touch
in dancing for fear of
falling into something
forced at best

and nor will it
nor can it nor should it exist
possibly, as a pistil
can not will itself
the grazing of bees.

While in daylight
I do not think of you

at night I lay with you
lapping my mind
thinking "please

consider my
breath on your neck
and your hand at my
throat could be more
than a tease."

Imagine one morning
we might wake up
and look at each other
in quiet and breathless
sighs of ease.

That this, in its frivolous
gesture between two
people whose paths
only cautiously
intersect

Could be that something
in avoidance of love
as we know not to seek it
but maybe for now
just sex

But we both know better
from mistakes of
our histories
and will continue to thrust
toward the edge

where we'll wait
and live in this desire

overlooking the mess
we could have made
if ever we wound up in bed.

Hamilton

I'm not entirely sure
when it happened.
It may have been the day after that one night
or it may have been that day when I couldn't not
what are you that makes such a
deep curve in my back
what are you to make my thighs flex upward
to what has not yet
what are you besides a spectator to my
slow steady decline
I'm going to haunt your future
as one who was never not yet
who was never yet entirely
I'm scraping sidewalks for spare cigarettes
and licking icebergs for crumbs
I forgot how lowly it feels to be less
than everything that has been passed
up
who am I
to shred the layers of dirty skin
to get to the sweet fruit
of what you had wanted
I'm not the darling saint
I am only the refugee
holding fast to the fences that keep me
in the right place
at the wrong time
your eyes are small and haunting
and this can't possibly end well

Kumquat

Crack me open
and sip of my juice;
lick the pulp of
my flesh and
devour my skin
with your teeth
until all that is left
is the heart of me.

But when you are done
have the decency
to plant me deep
in rich soil
so my treasure
can take root
and grow to bear
fragrant and heavy sweet.

When you do
remember there
is no way to replace
me to whence I grew
to the branches
that filled me full
to bud blossom
and seed.

Instead I'll grow
wooden bones
rooted deep
Where I'll gather the glow
of sun through tender petals
and make stronger
the ground beneath.

Juicing a Prickly Pear

What solemn splendor this
wanton and tender
desire for pain in pleasure
Where once was a gosling
now lies the treasure
of a golden goose's egg

How willingness can be
so passionate in fable
but lack all measure
of floral fragrance
that is loving

Tired this gooseflesh
how depraved in censored
liberty
where designed it is evil
bedeviled in wanting
and rejection fatigued

Ingenue strikes up in fallacy
Imagined weepings of willows
draw shade in fever
in craving of
compassionate reactions
of validity

Patterns emerge in imbalance
where hormones are left
uncontrolled but consoled
by those who don willingness
as the cape which lends to flight
night after night
after night

Pastry Display Case: An Erotica

Devouring a crisp croissant
that flakes and falls apart
just before it meets my lips
even when I tear it in tiny rips
or to reach out my tongue
to surround the slick
butter of gold pastry
into the pale blonde fluff
and melting cotton batter
is the warm rousing sexual
sensation I am after
more than any other pleasures.

Oh when I remember the
oiliness of my fingertips
fondling the sometimes chocolate
or candied almond atop
my mouth might water
or my heart might stop or
that little quake that starts
in my navel and extends
out into my arms and toes
could lead me to
begin to float
when I walk on two feet to it...

And I might dip it in my tea
or
bite it hard with my teeth
and let it flake a blizzard
all over the front of me
and frankly
it is genuinely preferred to the

laboring of learning new anatomies
or navigating seas of cock-sured
cuckolds dressed in vintage flannel
hoping to dismantle my carefully
curated and fairly substantial
self-assured willingness to
do only as I please.

And I like them when they're hot.
Steaming and shining in paper
or on white salad plates
paired with coffee or maybe
a pot of yerba mate
or sometimes a whole milk latte
if I'm feeling the seduction of cream.
May there be nothing more needed
to satisfy me
than a croissant, my pen, and some tea.

Hexagon

Love is pressing
honeycombs with
the tongue to the hard
palette without
ever considering
the violence of teeth

K-I-S-S-I-N-G

Oh to be kissed!
For the passion between
two lips overwhelms
the boundaries of
pronunciation
to instead succumb
to press
against those which
defy every definition,
bouncing bated exhales
against skin as they
dance, these lips
tasting every possible
sliver of flesh
until there is none left
to explore
and then again!

Til the salt has
all been licked
and tongues touched
slipping in flicks
blazing a new
wild landscape
in tender and sweet
or maybe teeth
might graze gently
and exchange caution
with possibility
and a hunger
for where it might lead.

The visceral taste of
loss of description
for this curious
boundless and freed
bliss
but what have we
left to sing of the
space left between
if not the premonition
of this charming
pleasure amiss
and to kiss
just to kiss
and be kissed.

Dummy

Wet pine
wrapped in brushed leather
tanned and oiled
and buffed once more
rippled and soiled
soaked in rosewater
rinsed in brine

Dancing

Have you ever tasted cream?
Before the fat is chewed swallowed and
Spat
Spitting for sake of spit
To switch and begin battle
But what's more to dance
Engendered arms outstretched and fingers
Inhabitants like little villages
Victorious erections on a horizon
Carved out with nervous nibbling
Tooth and nail

Invited she comes
a treasure of pillowed butresses and bustles
Under wide tanned leather
Stretched in daylong heat
What am I she
Screams behind privileged cow eyes
Where no vow had yet to breed

Quiet and sweet
A whispered reply
Under elbows and dropped hips of
Warm raw unpasteurized
Cream.
Shy and mistaken
To remind her
Of kismet indulgence in
Careless and crucified
Dreams. Sick grandeur.
Scarlet strobing cacophony
And wielded weaknesses
Left in flats
She left in

She does not speak

She sings.

Not louder than the diplomat
Wringing hands in prediction
Mystery under tags
In toes of shoes overworn
In tangled hair
And chipped teeth
Where it once lived this treasure
Now spoiled and spilling
Onto gifts worth more
Than the rhythm
And the sway
Or the pull
Come closer
Palm to hip
Shoulder and wrist
Pouring light off skin
In delight
Of the fleeting fantastical
taste of cream.

New Years Day

Once you were an ocean
and I a vessel in this
sea of sheets
and eyes left open
in absence of light
where our fingers carefully
traced our anxieties
on each others' skin

but in this darkness
you were a field of color
and a journey through
prisms of vibrance
unlike any other
body might harvest
as ripe fruit grown
sweet within me

A power of spirit
shapeless fragile
primitive and divine
beasts of pleasure we
created such
a complete current
of curious discovery
through synching beats

In darkness you
came to me
as a shelter and warmth
where the winters
chilled us raw and
roaring desperate rocking
us perfectly away
in tidal wave

Turmeric Ginger

Like exploring a new country
where all of the directions are in
a foreign language
using cashmere waves in wind
to follow the way to the salt sweet
sands of a lapping beach
Like the first taste of a new
spice or tea
navigating its path against
every taste bud
grazing sensitive teeth
not at all sure when to swallow
Like a great fabric of
bristle brushed cotton
folded and draped across
statues in the smoothest cream
and just enough current
to drown

Electric Yellow

In Absence of Bread and Cream

I think of her
often
the warm fresh breakfast
and pillow of bosom
peaking in tucked
apricot encouragement
she warned me
not ever to hurt her
and still I did
in a necessary and
hollow escape
to a paradise that would
never exist
I miss her
and the cream
of her perfect skin
untouched by sun
and dressed in silk
as she lay
where tears once dried
she held me
never had a love been
so pure and honest
in its shy
and timidly willing
calm tides of
perfection
I kissed her
and gave of her
my own zest and cinnamon
and honey forever
I promised
forever

I believed
until inflammatory winds picked
my pollen in flurries
and blew me
to such darkness
I could not see
the virginal beauty
that was she
in her delicate
gossamer veils of insecurity
so righteous
we tried
but the webs woven
caught me
and wound me tight
in a cocoon
I assumed to nourish
my growth
of wings
But in featherlight
biscuit and apple butter
she was my home
and without her I
am not whole
but lonesome in lacking
and craving for
what I so easily sent
back as if destroyed
Her turmeric ginger
healing to my ails
I did not share my
wild blooming chicory
nor let it grow in
her pasture of
amber sun-bleached
wheat

I coveted the lapping
beaches
at her bay
and sent her penniless
to coasts unblazed
where I promised her
freshwater waves
and delight
to our eyes had not
yet been seen
I loved her
and love her still
with new eyes
and fresh footprints
she will always be
the best part of me.

Angels in Hiding Because of Your Sins

there shall be no definition for this loneliness
which lies lonely in only
its relevance in caves and caverns
of exposed bricks and borrowed sheets
lack of permission
to abide by the definitions
for which you speak
laying lonely between sheets
sighing at voice-mails and unanswered calls
going through withdrawals
as if love is the only drug
I can't taste enough
to crave
He is the air that I breathe and I sigh in it
he is the water I drink and I drown
he is the food that I need that I crave
that I speak of
so humbly as if he is tea
against my swollen throat
my oxygen in need of sweet
breaths intangible among beasts
unfortunately
asking nothing of me
I am a treasure of temptation
I am a lion in heat
I am a swollen a swelling of meat
I am a healing of ill and a wet spot
on blankets unkempt for me
There are no apologies
sworn in my honesty oh yet question
and judge me please
I am your bait
I am your tease
I am the monster that haunts your dreams

In silences heavy in disruption
I am your treaty
I have brought nothing with me but peace
among my verses and waste
spoken in nervous haste
and a desperate cry for release
I am your danger manifested in cells
built only and unlucky for me
I am your worry your squander
I am your feet as your wander
in muck and the means to feed
Yet all in Hell is quiet as we
discuss our own needs
We cry and we scream
and wake up from our dreams
in borrowed sweatshirts and tees.
And what are you to me

Musings on a Light Switch of a Person

Forgive me of my breath
for you are a cold heart
and a warm tongue
where once there were a hand
to hold when my mistakes
were less extraordinary

Ricky

sick bitter chocolate
and sourdough
laced with
salt water memories
of iceans we never
drank of salt
only licked from
your freckled nape
and shoulders
and pancakes
I cried to
or sausage maybe
the morning my
heart wretched
in sobs my mind
denied over passing
evergreen tree lines
and an early vodka
that failed to
pause my briny
mourning of
loss before you
ever even fell.

What hell it is
to remember your
flaws so well
when you never
learned chance
to change.
And to miss you
is to miss a stranger
as I never met
the man who'd

fight to death
or fall to it.
But trees flooded
into 6am coffee
and the waitress
who watched me
burn my cheeks
at the thought of
losing you again
would never have known
I would forget.

2 New Messages

How just one word
can set off
a series of mazes
pre-planning phrases
that may be left
unsaid
tracing back
pen-strokes decoding
encrypted clues
unscripted
poring over references
of text messages
and the volley
of casual exchange
gauging a range
of emotion
playing each sigh
back in slow motion
wondering when exactly
you've changed

How hasty and
insignificant
these matches tend to be
while treasure chests
of truth and expression
hide underground in oases
of honest intention
far even from detection
of the sender
lies deeper the request
at stake
where maybe left
unanswered

the answer sought
might bait
another who happens upon
the perfect storm of
sentence structure
puncturing the thin rubber
holding water
left murky and deep
but only for me

The doubt and the silence
it creeps in between each
second passed after
the last pass is lobbed
while you
go right on
about your usual day
I sit here tracing punctuations
and spelling back
what you're really
trying to say
but the message delivered
I never truly considered
that maybe we ought
to go our separate ways.

Waking in Missouri

There are rocks in my shoulders
from carrying your negligence
like a satchel with one broken seam
such that my back might crack in
a weight of abandon and mystery

I am blinded from staring at screens
words written for reconnaissance
or at least the
acknowledgment
that we once existed in this dream

That our fairy tale romance
fleeting in bliss and naivety
was tangible and lucid as we
poured our souls over
caves and unsung melodies

On the road when you sat
eyes closed and musing
under gaslight and
vast pavement you spun me
high as you cried to me Sing!

Of beaches and linen
I sang to you swimming
in whiskey and ink and cream
our love was full bloom
and free

But in silence and absence
you hang dangling on fray
in fantastic apparitional scenes

of what we surely would
have been

A Modest Night with the Prince

Like waking up
from a dream you
were only the last bit of
salvation within me
holding me safe against
myself
where deep within
this
dark withered creature
waits for weakness
scaling the walls of
my humors and detestments
resentments
under fingernails peeled
and ripped where
once there had
been my testament
a claw to fend against
not for or to
but within my own voids
to spare them
sparring against witches
eeling their fingers deep
between my ribs
penetrating my lungs
as I clutch my
chest unknowing
if they are without
or within
But you had me
wrapped in arms
and pressed to your lips
my forehead red

and pulsing
from tears you
had not yet
learned to cause
as now they roll
you drink of them
like sweet water
proud to have found
the truest source
where the well can never
dry
tapping this trueness
this
unlimited fragrance of
desperation in beauty
that you might
truly
be my respite
but the fountain flows
without guard or levy
as I sit helpless
monsters make
a playground of my
wounds and abscesses
digging in and out
in double time
while you watch and smile
at the girl to
whom you could never lie
you've won
and you've left her shunned
in a pool of her own
filth and dismembered
trust
spin on your heel
and brush

the dust from your palms
your work here is done

Knife Fight or Flight

Maybe I'll press my cheek
to my shoulder for warmth
to feel the blood rush through my
own veins
from my own heart
to my own arms
to kiss and cradle my
own face
or my own mouth
might part and kiss my skin
where once it had been kissed

Maybe I'll light a fire
to my own self-esteem
to remind me of how you made me
own my own loneliness
unanswered calls
like mirrors to the desperation
in my tone I'm
losing feeling in my bones I'm
scattering ashes to waters that
aren't even my own I'm
tearing letters from words you spoke
I'm
trying to remember to set down my phone

But you're sweet
and you remind me
of the time I fell so deeply in
debt to your generosity
and charmed and catered speech
you surprised me
and showered down touches
and tenders so truly divine

from your pedestal got me
high enough to think I could climb
to be the one to lie
casually upon your chest
as if it was designed to be mine

And while faux and feigned
your performance is perfect
and seduced my misgivings
into hugging
the shadow of something
I've never been close enough
to to taste truly
loving
If an act I entertain it
for the play of love
still vibrates through my tendons
and tightening flushing skin
as if you are within me
and thank you
for lying so sweetly

for I'm not sure how deserving
of this love I might have been
were you to meet the me I was
then
or the me I have seen
twice maybe
and only in this dream
as the woman so glowing
in the light you shone
as if thrown to the sea she might
float on this beam at her
breast
where she said no in jest
but meant it

But only to stay you
here in this place where this
love could resist the pattern to fall
cease and desist
but in this
I can say that I love you
for the ghost you play with such care
the 'no harm done, darling's
the 'I'll always be there'

And rolling in sheets for one
fleeting and delicate treats
and treaties left unsigned in speech
undefined I own nothing
and have no right to keep
or acquire this
love before it expires.
But in plastic and facade you are perfect
and I will keep you here among rotted fruit
of loves long left in sun
but you are not the one

Oxblood

Better Than Anything Else That I've Tried

There isn't enough ice cream in the world
to make me feel worthy of care

washing the smell of cigarettes from my hair
and rinsing only to lather again 'til I am clean

like holding raw meat in vinegar and bleach
before marinating in its own filth for a while

trying to remember the bend of a smile
when I dream of felled bricks and concrete

I want only to wake up alone and feel complete
to love my own skin with reckless abandon

and to fall gently to sleep in the absence
of shoulders to gently cradle my cheeks

but at night is when this emptiness sneaks
into the cracks in folds of my belly and thighs

craving in desperation and silent dreaming cries
for attention or even subtle affection

without the pressure of taming an erection
that I never intended or for which had any use

closing my eyes and recounting unrequited abuse
of myself and of my own vices

burning blades or serrated verbal devices
against those I promised to love

including me
especially

but with only my own breath to breathe
and the carbon exchange of incenses

I dream of lives of princesses
dressed in gowns and princes and peas

no honest fragility has ever brought me peace
nor have the lambs ever stopped their screams

but vulnerable in sobs and tear tracks in ice cream
I may whisper 'now I lay me down to sleep'

Meetings with Angels

She doesn't remember whether or not it was
raining
the sting on her skin came from within
strict and unrelenting in its repentance
of sorrows fabricated in imbalance
She does remember the choking feeling of
demons
thirsting for vulnerabilities hungering for meat
their talons scratched at linings of arteries
as if without the blade she still might bleed
pouring into lungs desperate for reason to breathe
he cracked her chest open with two metal claws
snapping through rubber skin and gore
the crunch of bone and splitting armor
exposing tender bruises and spider spun fractures
from the last time she'd been captured
he needled through the bloat and waste
pillaging tumors scabs and teeth
fingernails blackened in blood and filth
he exposed her landmines and landfills
beneath rusting iron ribs and sour milk
and there she lay
inflammatory flesh and feminine rubble
rotting in her own undertow
dismembered and disemboweled in love
as her pulse began to slow
Your worth is greater than gold
he said as he washed his hands
of the spoils of the war in her breast
and placed her faults in his own chest
She doesn't remember why he left.

Blood Sausage

I package this shit of me
this shit of what had been that
sticks to my skin like leeches
sucking out confidence of character
I beg
do you laugh do you
at conscious recurring behaviors
you promised to give up
last Monday you trick
Quick hide your faults behind
fault lines you can't save enough to cross
bitter passenger
not best a traveler
unwilling to strengthen your
tendons enough to have a good laugh
at the tendencies
of bitter creatures like rodents
picking shards of broken people
and crushing them into carpets
to impale your tender comfortable
feet
wind your fabric tighter tighter
against your swollen hips
you fish
so accustomed to the bait
dancing lurid on hooks of treasure
kill you not for you appearances
if not bit at least
by a hunger for your substance of meat

An Hour Long Shower

I've been a forgiver in sainthood left ashamed in
some corner
of some studio I never really wanted to go to
And I look at it every day
these days
That tower of promises left behind
having stripped myself of my strong
because I knew I was going to cave in
and I didn't want to cave in
But it smiles in some sick yellowed
squared seductive anachronism
And each hair is slowly breaking
under stress of living
I have held my own needs close to me
and all of the nearest have fallen aside
and here he is just sitting there
working as we usually do
I'm forming a little terrarium
With only the dirt and the bugs I need
And he is a great big beetle
and his stake in land is generous
Here I don't have to hide
under strange moles on skin
I have yet to admire enough
to discover
It robbed me of my ability to say
It never actually happened
But it bestowed upon me
the blushing power to except
blame
My sainthood lies on the surface
of my weakening and cracking skin
and I haven't been taking good care
except for those who might see

Forgive and remember, I always say
but only in times like these
when hatred would validate me
as the weak
In my quiet terrarium
full of blood and the wake of monsters
I have no plans to speak.

Take. Eat.

Beasts be damned
to slaughter in
casual celebrated
violence
for only your flesh
may bring joy
brief and fleeting

Silenced screams
behind unmarked
blinders of concrete
as none who seek
your meat
should labor the
sound of your
last cries for mercy

A moment on the tongue
before gnashing
with teeth
for sustenance, purely
a generous source
of animal
protein

Christened in plastic pity
blushed swollen and fair
for this is
my body
at market price
bloodied with knives
served rare.

Whatever the Color of Misandry,
Navy Maybe

Always Having Shirts to Play Around In

What is it about
my countenance
that swells in you
that drags your
tongue against
your teeth in
passing inclinations
of passionate
imagination of
bodies tired
naked in fantasy?

Why is your skin
rigid and taught
in suggestion
I never had posed
in filled verbs
of supposed
permissions
you wrote left
unsigned by me

Contextually
praised positive
but only
for levity of breath
bathed in tonics
were we
to fulfill this
broad unnamed
fancy
where I obey
to your needs

You are suddenly
committed to
shade me
from the gazes
of those
you mistrust
competition in lust
without recognizing
my disgust of your
intent for never
I'd consent to be
your sow
slain in trophy.

Thank You. That's Very Kind

Every time I am called
sexy
without ever
contracting the eye or
parting my lips to
solicit your speech
the violence that coils
my fingers and flushes my
cheeks carves
half moons into my palms
and evacuates blood
from my heart with such
intensity that I might
not smile and respond
so graciously
and instead find strength
in pure misandry.

Beast in the Belly

I hate your deep delight
as I delight in it
dancing in a whirlpool
your skin is my water
and yet I am terrified to drink

Blueberry Rooibos

I'm breathing better now than I had before
and I'm going to blame it on you
but I'm going to remain thankful
for waking me to tea
and reminding me that I am not yet enough
even if enough
is what you consider me to be

Single. Female.

No gaze may steal mine
nor delight within me
the hope of a new
fancy.

Locked away in drawers
with hidden keys
there is a secret
history

It is only for me
never lent or shared
or possessed
in gluttony

something divine surely
or so considered
by those who
wish to read

or more to have read
skimmed in haste
to recite with great speed
what should be done with me

or better what role
they intend to play
in this performance of
catch and release

none may learn it
or recite it from memory
without plaguing in earnest
the very soul of me

and so it hides
in curtains as I sweep
to remain in dark
for no one to see

Ode of the Lonely Girl

I want to dirty my fingernails
in the mud and dirt
climbing a mountain
that no one else dared to climb
Rather than sinking them
into the skin
on the back
of someone who will never be mine.
I'd rather the scent
of roots and earth
fill my nostrils
with musk and pine
Rather than manufactured
bottled and plastered
cologne
of a man whose intentions hide
in lies
slick smiles
and burrowing smirks
I'd rather settle
into the love and affection
of the arms
I was gifted at birth
And with my lips pursed
I will sip of sweet fruit
and the truths laid
before me in color
I will be gracious
and grateful of
all that is given
without ever relying on another.

Streetlight

Prelude to the Blackberry Bush

I remember being little
never what I looked like
except for the view out and down
running around
in the mud and grit of march
and April
when the green gave its first try
but the early snow battled and won
for one or two or four more weeks
and our gloves were caked in mud
fingernails black and knees scraped
when we could finally take
our snow pants off
and play around in our jeans
and our noses would run
all over the yard
in debris from last night's windstorm
throwing peeled bark from sticks
or collecting moss for its feel
and we fed the fairies chocolate
they lived in the rosebush
and we made them gowns
in fabrics I don't remember
tiny violets hid in patches under
overgrown branches
in the shape of a dog's head
in tendon vines and budding fur
winding up the antenna
choking out the television
reminding us to go outside and play
in the mud and the toxins
and the poisons of dirt
we're just waiting to wash away

Nudity

Youth best in speaking such
ravishes ravishing
taut in their gazes of phrases unspoken
in tired wiry knots of thoughts
unwilling
unkempt
and in piles on floors from
where I was from
quietly
behind rose colored walls
into hallways of crooked jaws
and broken mirrors
and swollen tongues
emergencies in beds of weakening
lungs and circling bats
and witches breeding sages
of sage
of savages
in ruins of muck and maroon
and royal blue stucco it was
stucco her nursery
where we learned you
can't buy me love
where the mint curtains hung
where *Los Lobos* was sung
in offices of paid bills
and a mountain of dust
over books unread
while eyelashes curl behind
eyelids of hopefuls
in need of wardrobes
and the hooves they share
and in caring for white walls

and crystals she says
crystallizing around holes
for only silver and never gold
hollow haunts of a lover's moans
she never hears never
in silence and snores she sways
in love and misconscious
and warding against the obvious
as always
curling one dimple in favor
of another's submissive behavior
behind fiber wood doors
with 6 inches space above the
floor and her shoes
and I'm sure
and while tireless summers
will pass on in bugs
and in choking heat
and sunshine revenging
against winter's depressed
distressing it seeks
only your wonderful
in best lighting
and top sided shadows
on dimples of misguided
integrity
you're a whole of holes
and a sob of a story
who's won in one and its oneness
and lonely
and frailest of fairy tales
you are a shepherdess in sheep's
ware and in tears shed and only
wild in subterranean
tracks of trains too expensive
to ride backward

Meanderings of an Awkward Grey

And right now I'm sitting
In a pair of my mother's size 10
stink black
black jeans
in the back table
on the left of the room
behind three other tables
of the rich kids
in algebra
and all I can think about
is wearing matching
pajamas
in a room full of girls
on the lower floor
of some house
some Dad's business
had built
sparking inside jokes
to torment passers by
but they make fun of me behind lockers
one row down from mine
and I am never so close

Fine

Casual guise of
personal terror
and great
internal tragedy

thoughtlessly
greeting
strangers

pale and weak
or tiny things

so pretty

Girl, You'll Be A Star

Silence fills no voids
only bouncing
empty echoes of what
you probably should have
or would have
in time
or how you remember
the hollow faces
of passersby
or the vacant eyes
of strangers might
in instance so televise
your insignificance
so blindly
guess the figures
at which you used to balk
talking to walls and
chasing hands of clocks
where the steady steps
of listeners used to be
what once was your own
path to walk
and blink in sun
never paused or stopped
is now overgrown
with trees
behind glistening windows
where your reflection
may greet you
suites and suits and tailored
patterns for your dreams
dancing off lips of
the esteemed

guilt and greed
the happenstance that
your stance might happen
or your stake might stick
to ears and seed
black lace and satin
and backcombed frizz
cow eyes and pointed fingers
take careful measurements
and learn to behave
as her troubled temperament
she said so bold
and I shouldn't care
but I did
eat and they eat you
alive
where the porridge meets
the tips of tall branches
or the chip on your shoulder
becomes delicious
to monsters so malicious
you had better had never
find your voice in this desert
where we all still complain
about weather

Doyoumodel?

It's dark here
Predawn howling of coyotes
Stressed nostrils swollen in breath
Breathing less than the love by my side
And she doesn't know
How dark
It is in here

It creeps in darkness you know
The stickiness of heavy
The dead weight flanks of that heavy
That sick desperate heavy
When I can't see it
It screams through my sheets at me
And there is never enough light

I want the cool stinging pains
And sweaty dizziness
I want the fuzzy hollow
Of belly
Of where my bellies have been
Of the belly I sick
I want that sick hollow waste
Dizzy girls in high socks
Dancing pirouettes in sinewy
Silhouettes

In dark it rolls
Pressing the top of my panties
Resting in the deep crease of my hips
Hips spreading
Hips swelling heavy
Cushioned ball joints
Torn ligaments and
Bruisey shins

I never want her to know
This deep hollow
This heavy drawn belly
This sick dizzy fixture
That keeps me lit til light
This dark waste heavy
And heavy on me
Heavy hips

It keeps curtains closed
This dark
My hands and my heavy
While the chickens call for morning
And I can hardly breathe

High Fashion

The sexual nature
of frailness
and fantasy
submission
to veined hands
and stature

High-arching
hierarchies
of knowing
or to have
known one
who is something
greater than
the weakened wrists
of those who clasp
hands and
double kiss

May they well
hold rolls of
the souls of
sinewy thighs
and skin
sucked to bones

Ever present
in casual acquaintance
as much as
or more than
the unspoken
codes of phrases
or secret handshakes

in language
of service of
art for trade

How decadent
undeserved
desserts taste
to those who've
saved to savor
instead most
purchased in
grandeur never
a silver spoon
licked for flavor

A show of
monetary social
ease attracting
those whose
mouths and intentions
lie empty
save occasional
silver sparkling

When all wanted
is more money
they will have
it as predicted
prepared for
trade in wares
of flesh
restricted and
tightly dressed

Skin thick
enough to

go home
to studio
apartments in
places unknown
but thin enough
to know not
how to hear no.

Cactus, Maybe

Black Leather Jacket

What is it
about arrogance
that inspires
dress in skins of
beasts killed only
for the purpose
of dressing it?

Black Bagged

What is the feeling
of healing
to the sick who cannot
diagnose
her own sickness?
As a newborn cannot
discern its growth
when does a beast
become aware she
is owned?
What is it to learn
limits living
only mild?
Wildness of
the rabid is not
kenneled with reason
nor a foreigner
in recognition
of treason to kings
by whom they
were never ruled.
How does a fool
wandering in crowds
learn of his label
except by fable and
desperate fawning
or pawing to
entertain?
We remain lost
without light to follow
from hollowness of
being, for
darkness is only

in absence of rays
or floods of it.
How smoke
can be true to its fire,
a liar will worship
her secrets
in fear.
And in tears and
unclear objective
she directs
her own duress
to her misdirected
expectation of
tenderness.
Finding construct
in chaos
and changing winds
or tides
winds loose ends
to a knot
perfect and tidy.
Tidings of loss
fall on deafened
ears that never
knew what it
was to hear,
or eyes that never
learned to find
let alone to have lost.
Knowing not to
possess, having
owned all that
exists,
defines in effigy
the body of lies
wound tightly

around wrists
that knew not
how to resist.
For to follow
without knowing
to lead
is the blindness
that sheaths
our bound fists.
Her body might plead
"I cannot
nor will not
but won't stop
this spinning"
while standing
still in her own
misgivings,
unaware of her ills.
Even still
there is a whiteness
to her abject
objective in scarlet.
A target,
a destination,
for her energy to
be clean.
Not just to seem it,
but purely to be.
And though in
wild white wilderness
of scrambling of thoughts
in length
she is taught
her own weakness
in presence
of strength.

The Crippling Trap of Desire

Wanton and waning
and waiting for the right
moment to tuck what is
right beneath what feels
nice in order to get what
I want.
I want it therefore I will
have it. As if the stars will
align or by magic
what I crave in this moment
is what might save me
from the misery of
knowing that
somewhere in deep thought
or despair my wishes might
be granted. That my hopes
could advance it. That my will
and my worry and my planning
will give me the passage to
chance it and win.
That my own future might be
right between my own
fingers and schemes
and that I am the god
of it and create my own righteousness
for the one that I praise
which is me.

How worrisome a
consideration. How rightfully
terror stricken this thought leaves
me. I am nearly incapable
of standing properly

on my own feet
let alone find a beat
or remember when to eat
and yet I should trust only me?
That in the funny combinations
of phrases and stumblings
that rumble and tangle in
my speech there is an
all knowing omnipotent
relief?
When I am asked my spiritual beliefs
or my creed I try to conceive
a notion of false tendency
or misdirection. I
do not follow but
I certainly cannot lead.
And while some may
quite happily
fall to their knees
I find myself talking to
whatever it may be
from the seat of a chair
with my chin to the air
speaking quietly and only
to me.

Who else will listen?
Who else will care?
What is it within me that brings me
from terror to a place of peace?
I pray to be quiet.
To allow my mind to silence in
wants and disruptions
of arguments of ego
and constructions
without planned interruptions.

To let Me go.
For the craving and
crippling depravity
that inhabits my dreams
cannot be the God
I considered myself to be.
And when the wanting,
the wanton waiting for
what I want to appear
can pass,
I may have what I need at last.

Supernova

a sun
is a whirl of
residual fuel
from a combustion
of fire once
much brighter

harnessing
only a finite and
depleting memory
of once what strength
had been
bedeviled in
an eye blinded
by the light
of its history

maintaining in
arrogance
and illusion of
self sufficiency
what in slowness
feigns constant
in future is complacency

for what happens
when the burning
stops
if a halt of this
gradual regression
flaunts itself
in aggression of
darkness?

had it known all along
that there was nothing
new to burn
without the gift
or heinous cost
of fresh fire
would it ever learn?

Instead may it burn
itself in shame
seeking validation
of great loss
only to toss all
its former flame
in fear of going
dark again

it would masturbate
its own pity in
abandon and apathy
until coming
to considering the
possibility
of gathering new kindling
or accelerating
the embers left
with a source
outside itself

in willing
a new fire might
light within it
a new color
or breadth of flame
creating for itself

a new name
in its starlight
and brighter may
it beacon
on horizons
yet unreached

allowing itself vulnerable
the gathering of gases
and gifted tinder
and desperation
in presenting proud
its waning energy
to surrender
and serve
a new source
of steady light.

Fame

I have never given a performance
for ants that come into my apartment
looking for nourishment
and a change of scene,

but they probably watch
and complain that I
do a lot of picking at
my face and don't do more
with intention to entertain.

They probably say to each other
How foul, spending her
day eating lazily
and scratching with glazed
eyes, just sitting there
when she is on display!

Should she not dress
up for us, do a dance
maybe get up and play?

In fact sometimes I
forget that they
are trailing in lines under
the stove and refrigerator
and think not once
of my influence
on their children or their beliefs.

As spectators an audience
has no bearing on those

they observe
they have no power
or influence
no pivotal significance
to sway the speaker's words.

As eyes behind glass we
have no names
we are not relevant
except to those in our
way. But we huddle and
plot our own methods
to try to be the ones
on the stage.

Such is fame.

Such is the expectation of
prisoners and faces
we haven't yet
met though we know their
stories and names,
their histories and
greatest sources of shame.

We have created them
among us alone without
the precipitation on
their ability to reign.

For the ants might one
day find their
way to my ears
in my sleep and
blame me for the bait
of my dreams.

In that case I might
crush them
beneath my feet
without care
or respect to their
hopes to succeed.

All their lives might
end at my hands and yet
I will only take to paper
and pen and again
I might sit and eat
and write or read.

I will not entertain
those left to remain
having lost their
loved ones to me.

But as they still
wander through my
floors and window
sills they become
something of which
I am aware,
but I have the choice of
whether or not to care.

I might murder
them all with a mop
and not consider
their deaths a loss,
but even a gain.

And I might get
on my hands and knees
and strain my eyes
to find every last one
and deny them the ability
to abstain from opinion
of my fame.

Not for a purpose
or even as a show of
sheer power
but as a petal
might be picked from
a flower in simple
complete abandon
and apathy.

An utter lack of sympathy,
for their lives and opinions
of me are less than ignored.
They are never considered.

And while they all
had seen me and generated
their fear, as they scattered
from the spray the
day I cleared them of the space,
They all knew my face.

As a race of creatures desperate
to claim what was mine
they framed me as if
in a zoo. Watching daily
disappointed in what I
would do.

Well here in bed I lay
alone without threat
but considering
what destruction might ensue
when the powerful
realize their power
and take it as a weapon
and we are the ones
to be stepped in.

Olive

I wonder when calm
may become apathy
or when wilderness
becomes sacred space
for domesticity.

Lavender. Lilac. Chicory.

Tenants of the Trees

Dare you imagine
if the trees found out
how many lies
they breathe
or how many times
a lover's cry or moans
flew up through their
leaves
in selfishness
or vanity,
might they suffocate
or still wave
in smog and sun,
encouraged by tides
and the rhythm of
our evolution?

How need they not evolve
to accommodate
our deceptive nature?
Deceiving even the bees,
fostering them sweetly
to covet
their sweetness, soon
tossing the sweet away
once we have had enough
denying ourselves
as if they should be
punished
for creating such sweet
from beauty they
know not to keep.

As is the manner of
our wildness
as beasts,
collection without protection,
erecting statues
of ourselves
in honor of
our perceived greatness
and degradation.
How so great
as to flippantly
pass
and carry on in mirrors
without seeing ourselves
only eying those
seeking to keep us?
We shall not be caught!
Of course.

Entitled to breath
without gratitude
and nourished by
possession
of that which cannot
be claimed,
we human,
animal and disease,
cannot be slowed
or stopped
until we are caged
by that which
we gave no power,
but whose power
we casually
raped
with ease.

Romance with Jades

There is a color that used to exist
this
orange and violet that
my lines used to race to speak of
that my tongue wished to touch
to taste this
sinewy grape and froth
that is the sky over
intersections and towers
in the line of sight
at night
that color has been replaced
by a funny blue haze that sticks
to palm leaves as if
I have always been here
and I promised not to forget
to kiss each new leaf
as I passed
and to thank it for it's blessing
and grant it wishes
of appreciation
and foreign respect
but alas it's been months now
and occasionally I'll eye
a new limb or frond
and miss the way I
used to feel new
and used to nose the jades
and firm cactus
thanking it for being free
of who I once used to be

Nightwalk

Under the deepest indigo
in its over-worn gown
of tangerine lace,
place these feet.
A careful beating,
pulsing metronome plays
heart strings like
harpies, singing
heavy and silent
into this night.

Cool knees chill
in a trance of early
Spring's goodnight kiss,
missing the weight
of begging, bashful
cheeks,
but holding steady
pace in this
night as it creeps.

Wafting bitter
in newborn ever-
green and lemon,
delighted pine, and
needles of oleander
meander delicately
among petals dressed
in feigned moonlight,
illuminating paved
poverties of earth.

How blessed are the cursed
in this dimmed
damned gossamer of
shadow lazily tucked,
exhausted from dancing
in the waning lens
of eyes of the few passersby
in the silvery streets
of this night.

Bourgeois

Painted landscapes
in abstract verbs
tangible infrequencies
where tenants of labor
and swells of salt water
breathe vapor into
the spaces between
cells under duress
stress on syncopated frets
of fragrance in bloom
where night flowers
and subtle mint ice cream
meet in impression
or caricatured expressions
painted rust or red orange
buttery blonde and
electric blue delicious
but lacking in sweet
only to savor the grasses
forcing magic in crystal
and the dying of bees

Dillon

Had never so perfect
the sweetest aromas of
smoke without fire
extinguished echoes in
fuchsias and violent vibrations
meant less to punish
but to irrigate the soils
of souls left dripping
bathed naked
in panging vibratos
drowned in citrus and
coffee less foreign as
native to the grounds
where seeing is only through
pores sunken and filling
in color unlike anything
eyes might distinguish
so heavy must they
close to lather in lights
so careless, so free
oils of lavender and
kumquat trees shot
though veins deep
and rushing
tidal this sage
as waves of silver dance
through marrow of wooden
bones that could never
but grow

A Portrait of Wild Lavender

A heather of dust and green
but not quite green
as there is no better
combination of letters
for the ballet light dances
between
the furs
of softest creation
heavy coated dust
not collected no
clear intention
but true nonsensical
calliope of beauty so
sensual the cells
to the atom
fall to grey
so gently rippling
as laughter
at those who seek
to comprehend
as there could never be
a comprehension
of such a perfectly
wild thing

Amethyst.

Remember this peace
this calm in shifting winds
where nothing is to be considered
but the absent footholds
and ropes smoothed over
by sweat soaked palms

Had ever there been
water so still
as to not ripple even in tide
of sauntering moonlight
nor were life beneath
turbulent enough to wave

In this stillness thankless
and forgiven for its breathless
due expense or calamity
as if impending chaos
could be the only
viable excuse

Like crystal translucent
in pressure and weight
this is not pause
or absence of undercurrent
but the presence of allowance
for nothingness to hold its breath
and wait.

Bougainvillea

I live beneath
a curtain of fuchsia
flowers without
fragrance.

The petals they
fall to the pavement
showering in bright
the chain link and concrete.

In high kicking
high winds
they stick
to my windows

And as I approach
they signal
to me
I am home

But I despise them
for their lack
of sweet
or tart aroma

I wish for them sour
or citrus
as a rose or
peony might be

I want my
air of

my home
to fill with these
Hot pink excitements
a flurry or frenzy
of olfactory
delight

they anger me
nearly
in their arrogant
selfish slight of neutral

Do we not
deserve the
pleasure
of their smell sweet

Is this gift
solely
for the flies
or the bees

How dare they
assume they
are enough for me
in petal pinks

or the touch
of my fingers to
their soft
delicacy

or the bright
sunlight dancing
among their
falling leaves

or the various
species in
vibrant golds
and yellow greens
could possibly
satiate
my desire
to fully

experience
what it is
that might be
purest of beauty

No!
I despise it
for not rounding
complete

the sensual
voluptuous
experience
of smelling

I wish to
open my doors
to let it in
and flood me

even bitter
or pungent
why won't they
obey my needs?

For as their
treasurer
accounting their
pleasures

I fall to knees
and beg
why not I
am worthy

of tasting
through scent
their flushed
blush of wonderment

why so easily
they fall
without odor
or pheromone

what ground
can they claim
to own
on color alone

so I curse them
their frigidity
their aloof
apathetic essence

and I question
for what purpose
they grow
in my presence

White

The brightest
sun-soaked
white not
blinding but serene
bleached concrete purity
in absence of
filth this
subtle and constant
hum of white
low and hushed
as we were
so it was
in denial of theatrics
soft stucco
or pleasant plaster
less rays
than bathed
of light
never quite
ever seen under
lids closed in
passion
there
in its splendor
two white steps
in day
under a cloudless sky

Little Yellow House

There is no other
such gold
midday sun lit
ricocheting off
gentle swaying shoulders
in virgin champagne
tart.

No such crepe French blue
of a well worn sundress
the wind might waltz
beneath as if there were
no more darling place
to dance.

Vines or ivy or
limbs of ripe lemons
climb, envied by paint
on siding weathered
by such brilliant days
as this.

A thin layer of dust
cracked in several
layers of laquer
of comfort in home
of tapping dirt
off the bottoms of little
brown shoes.

What copper
or kindling sawdust
sparkle ablaze is it

that dresses such sparkling
and how dare one carry
vibration so bright
on statuesque
marble laced in this
golden light.

Angelic and welcoming
as a gate to clear
to the purity of discovery
of hidden ills
no greater still
than the precious
gem of clean.

Muse in All Floral

This vibration
under my sternum
where night blooming jasmine
and orange blossom
take root and fertilize
what has been
so decently wrapped
Muse she coos
the sorrows and shame
that built foundation
of my bones and set my
blood to flame
where once was prohibited
sanity this
dedication against reason
became peaches filling
and expanding in flavor
to be juiced out of season
oh nectar sweet in splendor
and so heavy in its
syrup and golden delicious
less stern as honey
satin tonguing
hidden letters, tart and sinister
savoring malice
palatable and smooth
as if sugar laced in
reckless fiction
were capable of telling truth

Late Winter

2:17 in My Bed Without Them

I've come far too far to
polish these arms through
tool and anguish of hatred
for the words I've been lied to
with three or four tries

I'm cold in the absence
of warm down and laughter
through muffled rubs of thighs
and entrails warm in delight

Without which my blood won't
bother to boil
Toiling in banter of masters in
their quiet kin
their willowed peaks
their widowed sneaks
and all of the down trodden listeners
of lies through teeth

But the shallowest of creeks
harbor crawfish that feast
on bait we've not laid in years
Drinking our tears they lie stronger
and crave us much harder
than any of the mouths we let breathe.

Nomad's Widow

Kind widow sits at cold windows
pressing her skin against
the glass as to feel him again
whispering fog to the
smooth frosted pane
slippery fingers glide
dancing in breath
of all the things
she missed
perhaps an eye might catch her
pressing her lips to her breath
dancing fingertips
fawning consideration
for what else might be
passing inside
Kind widow wears her finest perfume
and laughs at the blinks
though entirely preoccupied
as her own
a slow soft windmill of jasmine
and rose for moonlight
she will never feel him on her
neck again
grazing knuckles kneading her gently
as her eyes begin to close
her cheek presses cool
where he once left an imprint of his lips
kissed only by the smoothness
of the pane
Kind widow whispers to her lover
the loss which is not yet
she dances
in clouds of smoke

and wails from crowded rooms
and presses her fingers to windows
and feels him again

Tim Wants to Be a Hummingbird

Tim wants to be a hummingbird.

Locket. Tommy-gun

He arches his
shoulders back
birdlike
silverback
lifting
wondering
what his
body speaks
if ever it does
as his eyes
fall useless
entranced
behind lids half
lifted half
shyly though
wilted in age
hushed down in bass
synching
yet fitful
elbow to waist
sipped synth
sieved and settled
forearms snake-like
winged beasts
as he might be
where once
winged he
feigns angelic
makes angels
jealous
of purity

Arts and Crafts

I want to glide
my bitten fingernails through
piles of half dried acrylic
paints and smear it over
the view of the world I've
etched out in vain.

I want to throw it
like bombs
into the hair of those who
love me and squish it
in my fist with fury
and grit my teeth

the brightest cerulean
I want it
under my feet and stuck
in the creases behind my boney knees
I want to roll my skin
in it soft nude

I want to holler like
a devil in heat to ceilings
too high to
pummel with
bloodied blue knuckles
as I'd wish it to be
and throw glitter
like shrapnel shimmer
into the eyes of my enemies

I'll smear ink on my
face to signal war

against myself and beat my
chest with lime green palms
and open my eyes wide
to shriek my throat raw

crepe paper missiles
in pink and black and gold
shooting across an empty room
and hanging on walls or
in windows
thrown clumsily by me
bombing lands of hardwood
trudged with bare feet

watercolor soot and
pastel violet fingerprints on the
noses of my friends
dipped in metallic silver
their fingers and toes
leaving trails on doors
and their knobs so I know
where they go

Sitting naked vermillion
electric white and tangerine
rolled up in confetti and
pipe cleaner dreams
wrapping yarn into spirals
and mumbling of my needs

I am perfect.

if you need me come find me
I'm warring in the art of me
as the heart might war
with the fingers or pen

but painted in vibrant and
violence of pigment
as my mind knows only to read
but has not yet learned to speak.

Butter

Stand quick sweet
Shear your legs for
the cream rises to the top
you know
Where were you with your
shrill beckonings for solace
when I was in the driest dust storm
piling ashes upon dunes
as if it hadn't been already
Does it stick to the hairs that grow timidly
out of your lip
Does it silence you when your breath
longs for toxicity
Does it fall into the pores on your cheeks
when you whirlwind your dirt
toward me
Stand in your own path
my sweet cry for deliverance
come take my hand into the quicksand
swallowing my feet
take hold of the grass at your ankles and
pray for your next
sweet
inhalation
Sieve your curd and spill your milk
your silence is spoiling

Harley not Charlie

had not a will
born so softly to green soaked
darkness
so tightly packed in
in wool
and brushed cotton
been passed as favorable
in passing favors
and dancing in twelve
by twelve inch floor space
for one
as if for two might bring
intimacy where shoulders
checked and fingers rolled
and licked to so
engage was it
had not we
had been
completely distracted
by tossed blonde hair
and how dare she
why maybe
why not yes
soles pressed against glass
in harmless disrespect
surely then why doubt
the intentions of beasts
feeding their noses and beaks
and mounting
in tattooed mouths of pretenders
as she
for instead
where had they been

Brady Street

what have you done
shills and harlots
maybe we are just
a swollen a swelling
a mass of seduction
in
some lost integrity
don't you know I've felt this
don't you know I've been this
deep
once upon a time
this speech
swarming with questions of treats
sweets
dearing my darling my soul swelling
wanderer
silence your stories your words do not
bore me but still
sitting at the sill of a window
asking the loud streets to still
my wandering
my will of suggestion
to remind your oppression
of checks and their common fees
sit in your worry
you melt
a hand at your belt and a sob
fingering your pockets for keys
question your willingness to speak
and sit in your
quand'ries
along in your wandering in streets
sorrows for those which you sneak

hide in your caves of
creations
and spar your aggressions
with armies of
follicles thick with strawberry hair
you're still sweet
you're still
in your stillness
ask me no words while I mention
you're childish aggression
and harboring
where are your cells when you speak it
where are the trees you were climbing high
in submission to thousands of failed tries
skip your common
skip to the loo
where were your memories of
all of the sadnesses previous
where have you been holding us
why are you climbing
so high
above us
swim in your squander
and bow to your judicial manners
tattered coats and stretched seams
we all have our histories
built into thread we found in our drawers
of all of our forgotten things
and Ice was my enemy
the piles of runoff frozen into icebergs
on streets
and this street was the most dangerous street.

Cafe Con Leche

Not the Evil Twin

He was a lion
A slow stalking pride
bellowed velvet he spoke
usual genuine
occasional dramatization
heavily peppered in
fuck
The softened skin below
salted follicles
his jaw
showed his forty years
His body broad and soft
He was a bear
I would impale
to save my own life
His zygomatic strength
and temple-hugging clenches
gifted his temper
fair warning
Never angry
His silence a heavy blanket
insulating your cold
shoulder

Tickets to Thailand

Darling did you once
fall into the arms
of a tree
out wide and contoured
so perfectly
just for me
did you wander
where the bark met the meat
where the sap ran thick
and fragrant
beneath withered and sunstruck leaves
how dare the air swell
like rolling plumes of debris
sticking in salt
and sliding in grease
to the space where the shoulder
blades meet
pressing skin to smooth brown grey
slowly rising to low clouds
and peaks peeking through sunrise horizon
leaving dents and scratches on cheeks
kiss him once for me

10/10/10

I'm beginning to look
just like my mother.

Women writers have poured
their hearts out
since nearly the dawn of
our expression
mourning the day
their faces begin to sink
into the trails and freeways
laid out by the bearers
of our creation.
The women whose
bodies they picked apart
in front of us,
whose insecurities
became our own,
become a mirror image
of our own evolution
into the women they
trained us to be.
The way my mother's skin
dimpled and stretched
and tore for me
became her biggest source
of personal resentment
or jealousy,
as she traced where they
cut her and folded her,
where the cravings I gave
her landed and grew
ravenous adipose
tissue that
could never be tamed

back to her former frame.
It was me.
Before I knew how to
find disgust in my saddlebag
hips she blamed me for the
ones she carried.
Before I learned to
disguise my bruisey
shins in stockings she
pulled hers into hose and
asked if I could still see the
"bulletholes" left from
years of being clumsy.
That, too, she passed
on to me.
As a child I looked
down at my little full belly
and learned to find it ugly.
She would grab at her ribs
and say "see, this is what you
did to me"
with a smile always,
but the fact of the matter
was easy to see.
It was because of me.
I mangled the body of
a true stunning beauty.
I wonder sometimes
what I might have thought
of her were she not
to tell me only what she
wished she could reverse
had she not had me.
"I used to model" she'd
say, showing me pictures
of herself

as a slim size 2 or 3.
She was 32 when she had me.
And here I sit still without
children, skin
falling rapidly from the
height of our cheeks.
Creases from our smile
carved into the corners
of my eyes,
my mouth framed gently in
ravines.
But most beautifully
I see my lips.
Slightly slanted upward
to a ridge rounded and wide
that lifts in the center
when I smile big and
toothy.
The smile she
gave me.
To weather any storm
and head-on face the
world despite what war is
going on inside of me.
This funny fold of
pink that tucks under when
I grin,
the warmth of my skin
the coffee mixed in cream,
the eyes that can't
help but emote even
when we're pretending
to be clean.
When I look in the mirror
I see her
staring back at me.

Truth and lies
and overwhelming
insecurity.
But within it there is this
power
a source I can't
yet explain.
This stone and redwood
strength that I imagine
her mother carried.
And passed along we
are concentrations
of generations of
lives we've grown
to breed.
Each one more aware
of the tangible differences
and similarities.
The lines in
our fingers and
our little moles.
The way our collarbones
show when we're starting
to feel skinny.
There is a power
in the bones underneath.
There is a universe of knowledge
and beauty bestowed from her
upon me.
And I am forever
grateful.
And lucky.

Cafe Con Leche: A Self-Portrait

diluted espresso
and heavy cream
dusted in chocolate
maybe casual pour of sugar
stirred lazily
foam left freckled
in muddy moles
of cocoa
held for warmth
briefly settled
as not to burn the tongue
but probably sipped
too soon anyway
in lasting punishment
then set aside
until cold and abandoned
swigged later in haste
for a fleeting
moment of pleasure
celebrated only
for effect then
casually tossed aside
maybe purchased again
when convenient

Grape and Froth

"Color"

I loathe the word "color"
for the purpose of defining
the dissection of light as filtered
against the structures and energies
of vibrations in ether.
How dare it
"cah" so abruptly on the soft palette
and "uh" so lazily as if to scoff,
as "coming" opposes the
mutual and symphonic tremor of
a blessed and treasured
"orgasm."
It is defining a Rapture!
A perfectly orchestrated
marriage of light and
energy,
drawing to it yet more light
in vibrance and forte
the brighter the contrast be.
Its only redemption lies in
its height and tongue to teeth
tapping "l" which seductively
allows the mouth to taste-feel
it's proper luxury
and linguistic liquidity.
Yet still bland in
flavor, "or" leaves us
nothing left to savor;
Instead it leaves the
mouth rare and raw
without properly cooling
or quenching our
thirst for more.

This language lacks such
cunning as the senses explore
in our dimension of
ambient perception.
How must "color" be
the chosen, petted;
unfettered or questioned
pattern of compulsory
designation for such pure
and overwhelming beauty?
Or rather, what letters might
do us much better?
Switches and quicks so
delicious on the tongue, crunching
traitors and inquisitive suggestions of
consent to the flow
of breath from throat teeth.
Guttural and grotesque
or mushing in muddy maternal
milks and majesty,
could the cut of the
"c" carry the awe and odor of
aural dances of olfactory
romances in cacophonous
homophony of ensembles of
winds?
Or rather, to seek such
inhibited direction to define
an incomprehensible
intention, should definition
lie back in submission
to letter and speech?
Hath nature to speak
would it mention
the flurry of light,
balance, and reflection

on leaves?
Or would it simply
just
be?

My Own Shade of Violet

The only thing left
that is mine
and mine only
is the color I see
when I speak
or you speak back
to me.

And for that I am
lovely.
Among other things
that remind you
of someone else
surely.

And I will never
share with you
the taste of my
froth orange raspberry
So I will have left
my me for only me

even as I share
my deepest
lovelinesses
and tactless tales
of wounds I carry
in my sleeves.

And I sleep soundly
knowing you will
never see
my tangerines

my violet berry
and olive greens.

Not a verse
nor a single word might
haunt you as they
haunt me
or taunt you
into belief

that what I see
is what I see
and it is only for me.
No less care have I
what care it is you
have bestowed in these

shades of autumn
cocoa and cerulean
Dappled with my
intention my own
vermillion memory
that live within only me.

About the Author

Elyse Michele Cizek was born in Los Angeles, California and raised as the awkward and middle child of a mixed family in the small town of Delavan, WI. She studied Creative Writing at the University of Wisconsin-Milwaukee where she found poetry to be the most effective outlet with which to process her depression, narcissism, and alcoholism. Currently residing in Los Angeles, California, Cizek is also a licensed esthetician, avid singer and songwriter, and spends her free time taking care of other people's cats.